PRAISE GOD
with
PUPPETS

BY ANITA REITH STOHS

ILLUSTRATED BY
MICHELLE DORENKAMP

SAINT LOUIS

With thanks to my mother, Elsie Roschke Reith, for giving me flour paste and paper to use for making stick puppets from Tinker Toys; to Leah Serck for showing me how to use puppets creatively in religious education; and to Sarah Musgrove and my daughter Miriam for field-testing many of the puppets in this book.

All Scripture quotations,
unless otherwise indicated,
are taken from the
HOLY BIBLE, NEW INTERNATIONAL VERSION®. NIV®.
Copyright © 1973, 1978, 1984
by International Bible Society.
Used by permission of
Zondervan Publishing House. All rights reserved

Cover designed by Tamara Clerkley CPH

Copyright © 2002 Anita Reith Stohs
Illustrations © 2002 Concordia Publishing House

Published by Concordia Publishing House
3558 S. Jefferson Avenue, St. Louis, MO 63118-3968
Manufactured in the United States of America

1   2   3   4   5   6   7   8   9   10   11   10   09   08   07   06   05   04   03   02

CONTENTS

INTRODUCTION

Bring a puppet into your classroom and watch students' faces light up with enthusiasm and anticipation. Puppets add action to any story. And when you use them as you tell Bible stories, children will listen attentively and will readily visualize and remember the Gospel message.

Children like to get involved in puppet plays as well. When you involve children in making puppets, working out dialogue, and giving a puppet show, you provide them with a learning experience that will stay with them long after they have left your class.

The easy-to-make puppets in this book are constructed with materials that are readily found in your classroom, home, or local craft and discount stores. Each idea is accompanied by directions and sometimes patterns. A Bible story is suggested for each puppet idea. But don't stop there. Use them with other Bible stories or create your own Bible story puppets and plays.

The God who made our marvelously diverse world and each individual in it is a creative God. Use puppets to celebrate the God-given gift of creativity with the children you teach, allowing them the freedom to experiment and create their own puppet figures and plays as they find new ways to praise God with puppets. There are as many ways to use puppets as there are ways to make them:

1. Make puppets before teaching and use them as you tell the story. If it's appropriate to the story and the kind of puppet you've made, have children hold the puppets to review the lesson.

2. Have each child make a puppet to use in a Bible story review or in a presentation to another class.

3. Have each child make a set of puppets to take home for telling the day's Bible story to someone there.

4. Make puppets to represent contemporary figures to use in acting out story applications.

5. Use puppets in morning devotions in the classroom, weekly chapel services, Sunday school openings, or special children's services in weekend worship.

6. The materials suggested in this book are just the beginning. Be creative as you gather materials for making puppets.

The puppet ideas in this book come out of more than 25 years of teaching children from preschool through middle school and teaching a class of young adults with developmental disabilities. The purpose of these puppets in such teaching has been to witness to the story of God's love to us in the Bible, with its ultimate fulfillment in the death and resurrection of our Savior, Jesus Christ.

My prayer is that through the power of the Holy Spirit these "Good News puppets" help you and the children you teach grow in understanding of the wonder of God's forgiving love and grace.

Praise God!

ANITA REITH STOHS

STAGING SUGGESTIONS

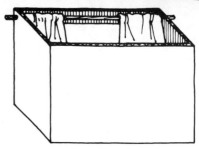

TABLETOP STAGE

Place a piece of drawing paper, poster board, shelf paper, cardboard, wrapping paper, or vinyl on the surface of a table or desk. Use markers to draw in stage details. Move puppets over the paper as you tell the story. Can be used with any stand-up puppet.

STAGE CURTAINS

Cut a piece of fabric to fit the width and height of the box stage opening; add several inches to the width, plus two inches to the height. Cut the fabric in half vertically so the curtain can be parted in the center. Fold over the tops of the fabric pieces and sew or glue a casing in each. Slip a dowel through the curtain casing. Cut holes for the dowel in opposite sides of the box so the curtain will hang inside the box in the opening. Fit the stick in place. Can be used with any open top and open bottom box stage.

BOX STAGE WITH OPEN TOP

Cut off the top of a corrugated box. Cut a stage opening on one side of the box. Decorate the outside and inside of the box to look like the setting of the Bible story you will tell. This stage is suggested for use with marionettes or with stick puppets that have the stick attached at the top.

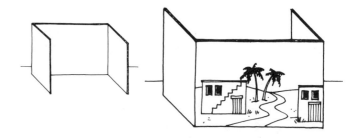

THREE-SIDED STAGE

Cut the top, bottom, and one side from a box so it has just three sides. There will be an opening at the bottom so you can hold the puppets inside the stage without your hands being seen. Decorate the box as you wish. Position the box stage on a table so you can move puppets above the edge of the stage. Place a large, three-sided box directly on the floor to sit behind. Can be used with any stick, hand, or finger puppet or marionette.

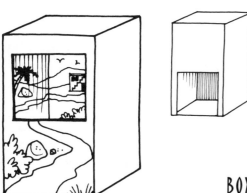

BOX STAGE WITH OPEN BOTTOM

Using the illustration as a guide, cut a stage opening near the top of one side of a box. Cut a stage entrance near the bottom of the opposite side of the box. Decorate the outside and inside. Place the box on a table or desk. Puppets enter the stage through the opening in the lower part of the back of the box. Can be used with any stick, hand, or finger puppet.

STAGING SUGGESTIONS

CARD TABLE STAGE

Turn a card table or other folding table on its side. Drape it with a sheet or table cloth. Sit behind the table and hold stick or hand puppets over the top to perform the play.

CEREAL BOX STAGE

Cut all around the sides of the cereal box, six inches from the bottom. Cut a small opening in the bottom of the box. Cover with construction paper. Hold the box with one hand while you put a puppet through the opening in the bottom of the box. Can be used with any stick, hand, or finger puppet.

PAPER PLATE STAGE

Cut a slit across the middle of a paper plate, but don't cut it completely in half. Draw or glue a background above and below the slit. Insert small finger or stick puppets through the slit to act out the story.

MILK CARTON STAGE

Cut the top and bottom from a small milk carton. Wash the carton so no milk residue remains. Cover the sides with construction paper and draw any needed details. Hold the box with one hand while you put a stick or finger puppet through the opening to present the story.

ENVELOPE STAGE

Cut a stage opening in the front of an envelope. Draw the background scene on the envelope. Cut a slit along the bottom of the envelope. Seal the envelope. Slip stick puppets through the slit in the bottom to act out the story in the opening.

STYROFOAM TRAY/EGG-CARTON STAGE

Turn over a Styrofoam tray or egg carton. Push stick puppets through the Styrofoam to stand them up. Move the puppets from beneath the carton to act out the play.

PAPER BAG STAGE

Cut a stage opening in one side of a large brown paper grocery bag, shopping bag, or gift bag. Draw the stage background or glue on construction paper details. Slip hand or stick puppets up from below to act out the story.

STICK PUPPETS
PAPER PUPPET

What You Need

White paper

Crayons or markers

Scissors

Glue

Craft stick

What You Do

1. Use the patterns on the next page to trace or photocopy figure, or draw it freehand.

2. Color and cut out the figure.

3. Glue a craft stick to the back of the figure.

4. Hold the figure by its stick as you tell the story.

More to Do

1. Cut puppet characters from old lesson leaflets, newspapers, magazines, or pictures downloaded from the Internet.

2. Make a classroom set of basic puppets to use throughout the year.

3. Cut figures from construction paper, wrapping paper, poster board, or fun foam (use craft glue to fasten sticks to fun foam).

4. Trace or photocopy puppet shapes for students to fill in with their own drawings.

5. Glue paper figures to poster board or cardboard. Laminate for more durability.

6. Enlarge puppet patterns. Glue large poster board figures to dowels or cardboard tubes.

7. Turn over a Styrofoam tray or egg carton and push sticks through, or push sticks into a ball of oil-based clay, so puppets will stand.

Production Possibilities

• Use around a classroom table with a small box stage or three-sided stage.

• Large figures attached to dowels can be used with a card table stage.

• Give each child a puppet to hold as he or she helps read or tell the story.

• Have children take home a puppet set and a stage made from a paper plate, envelope, paper bag, cereal box, or milk carton to use in telling the Bible story with their families.

The Lesson Connection

Jesus and the Children: Matthew 19:13–14

Have each child in the class make a stick puppet to represent him- or herself to hold as you tell the Bible story. Gather the puppets around the Jesus puppet as you tell how Jesus wants all children to come to Him. Thank Jesus for loving all children, young and old.

Paper Puppet Patterns: Jesus and the Children

Patterns may be used this size or enlarged to fit your needs.

ENVELOPE PUPPET

What You Need

Envelope

Craft stick

Glue

Markers or crayons

Scissors

What You Do

1. Seal the envelope, and draw a figure or scene from a Bible story on one side.

2. Cut a slit in the bottom of the envelope, and glue the end of the craft stick inside.

3. Hold puppet by the stick to tell the Bible story.

More to Do

1. Make a two-sided puppet by drawing a second scene on the back of the envelope. Turn the puppet as needed to communicate the story or biblical concept.

2. Use different colors and sizes of envelopes for different scenes in the story.

3. Use colored index cards instead of envelopes, and glue a craft stick to the back of the card.

4. Stick the craft stick into a ball of oil-based clay to make a tabletop puppet.

Production Possibilities

- Use for small-group presentations around a table. Staging options include a small box stage with open bottom, three-sided stage, or stage made from a cereal box or milk carton.

- Large mailing envelopes can be used for large group presentations. Draw puppet faces on envelopes and attach them to dowels or paint sticks.

The Lesson Connection

Jesus Stills the Storm: Mark 4:35–41

Draw a boat horizontally on each side of an envelope. Draw smiling disciples in the boat with Jesus beside them. Add low waves below and beside the boat. On the other side of the envelope, draw high waves around the boat with disciples who are afraid. Make a stick figure puppet for Jesus. Move the boat back and forth as the storm rises, turn the boat around and increase the rocking. Use the Jesus puppet to tell how He told the wind and waves to stop. Turn the boat back and slow down the movement as you tell how Jesus has power over the wind and waves. Thank Him for His love and care.

DRINKING STRAW PUPPET

What You Need

Paper

Markers or crayons

Scissors

Drinking straw

What You Do

1. Using the pattern on this page, or one you have created yourself, draw a figure onto a piece of paper. Include tabs at the top and bottom of the figure.

2. Color and cut out the figure.

3. Cut a slit in each tab.

4. Fit the straw through the slits in the tabs.

5. Hold the drinking straw and slide the figure as you tell the story.

More to Do

1. Omit the slits and tape the figure to a drinking straw.

2. Cut tabs at the sides of the figure. Cut a slit in each tab and slip the straw through. Slide the figure back and forth as you tell the story.

Production Possibilities

- Use for a small-group presentation. Possible stages include a box stage with open bottom; three-sided stage; or a stage made from a paper plate, paper bag, cereal box, or milk carton.

- Have each child make a drinking straw puppet to take home so they can share the Bible message with their family.

Drinking Straw Puppet Pattern: Jesus

Pattern may be used this size or enlarged to fit your needs.

The Lesson Connection

Jesus Ascends into Heaven: Luke 25:50–53

As you tell the story, move the puppet from the bottom of the drinking straw up toward heaven. As an option, make a paper plate stage. Draw disciples at the bottom of the plate and a cloud across the top. Cut a wide slit below the cloud and a small slit at the bottom of the plate where disciples are standing. Insert the drinking straw into the slits and pull the Jesus puppet through the top slit as you tell the story of his ascension. Remind the children that Jesus is always with us, although we cannot see Him.

11

STICKER PUPPET

What You Need

Stickers

Craft sticks

What You Do

1. Buy a set of stickers that illustrates the lesson you want to teach. Religious stickers illustrating a variety of lessons are available at Christian bookstores.

2. Place each sticker onto the end of a craft stick.

3. Hold the stick as you use the puppet to tell the story.

More to Do

1. Turn a Styrofoam tray upside down and stick the end of each craft stick into the tray to stand it up.

2. Stick the craft stick into a ball of oil-based clay to make a stand-up puppet.

3. Attach the sticker to thicker paper, cut around it, and glue it to the craft stick.

4. Place stickers on fingertips or on the ends of glove fingers. Move your fingers as you tell the story.

5. Paint craft sticks or use colored craft sticks.

6. Attach stickers to drinking straws or pencils.

7. Cut index cards in half, attach a sticker to each half, and glue a craft stick behind it.

Production Possibilities

- Use for small-group presentations with each child holding a sticker puppet.

- Suggested stages to use are a small box stage with open bottom; three-sided stage;

or a stage made from a paper plate, envelope, paper bag, cereal box, or milk carton. Decorate a stage with other stickers to help create a background.

- Have children make a set of sticker puppets to use in telling the story at home.

The Lesson Connection

Creation: Genesis 1

Buy stickers of celestial figures, such as planets and stars, as well as objects found in nature. Place each sticker on the end of a craft stick. Place the sticker puppets, one at a time, into the back of a Styrofoam tray or ball of clay as you tell the story of how God made the earth and everything in it. Or make a cereal box stage and use additional stickers to show the heavens and the earth. Each time you introduce a new object, say a thank-you prayer. End by thanking God for making each of you His very own.

SUCKER PUPPET

What You Need

Stick suckers

Paper napkins

Rubber band or string

Fine-tip marker

What You Do

1. Unfold a napkin and place it over the sucker "head."

2. Wrap a rubber band or string around the napkin in place below the "head."

3. Use markers to add eyes and other details to the face.

4. Hold the puppet by the stick as you tell the story.

More to Do

1. Use a white napkin for the base of the puppet, fold a colored napkin over it for the puppet's robe.

2. Make a larger puppet by placing a dowel inside a Styrofoam ball and covering it with a large piece of tissue or fabric.

3. Place puppet sticks into a ball of oil-based clay to stand them up for a tabletop presentation.

4. Have each child make a white angel puppet for use in telling Bible stories that include many angels.

5. Use yarn instead of a rubber band or string to tie around the napkin.

6. Omit the sucker and use the rubber band to fasten the napkin to your finger.

Production Possibilities

• Use for a small-group presentation with a small box stage with open bottom; three-sided stage; or stage made from a paper bag, cereal box, or milk carton.

• Have children make puppets to hold for an around-the-table presentation.

The Lesson Connection

Angels Appear to the Shepherds: Luke 2:8–14

Have each child make an angel puppet to hold as you tell the story. When you tell how the angels announced the Savior's birth (they sang to the shepherds), have the children sing the following verse to the melody "Jimmy Crack Corn."

Glory to God in highest heaven;
Glory to God in highest heaven;
Glory to God in highest heaven,
And peace to all on earth.

3-D PUPPET FACE

What You Need

Construction paper

Scissors

Pencil

Glue

Jumbo craft stick

What You Do

1. Using the patterns on page 15, trace face features onto construction paper. Cut a face, beard (optional), eyes, and nose.

2. Fold the nose in half along the center. Fold up the nostrils and glue the nose onto the face so it projects slightly.

3. Cut and glue on a construction paper mouth and hair.

4. Glue a jumbo craft stick to the back of the face.

5. Hold the puppet by the stick as you tell the story.

More to Do

1. Glue on yarn for hair.

2. Use movable craft eyes.

3. Draw the face with markers. Cut and glue on the 3-D nose.

4. Cut holes for eyes. Hold the puppet to your face to use as a mask during storytelling.

5. Cut strips of paper and curl them around a pencil or pull the paper, with your thumb on top of it, over a *dull* scissors edge. Glue on the curled strips for 3-D hair.

6. Glue on a cloth headpiece or metallic paper crown.

7. Tape or staple large puppet faces to the end of paper towel rolls or oatmeal boxes.

Production Possibilities

· Make small puppet faces for small-group presentations; use larger puppet faces for medium- to large-group presentations. Stage options include a three-sided or card table stage.

· Let each child hold up a puppet face and speak for it in a readers' theater presentation.

· Use large puppets for a church sanctuary presentation of the day's Bible readings or for chapel, a special children's program, or worship service.

The Lesson Connection

Jesus and Nicodemus: John 3:1–21

Vary the size and color of the beard to make puppets to represent Jesus and Nicodemus. Give Nicodemus a head covering that shows he had wealth and stature. When telling the Bible story, hold a puppet in each hand as you tell how Nicodemus learned that "God so loved the world that He gave His one and only Son" as Savior (John 3:16). Ask the children to tell what God's love means to them.

3-D Puppet Pattern: Jesus

Patterns may be used this size or enlarged to fit your needs.

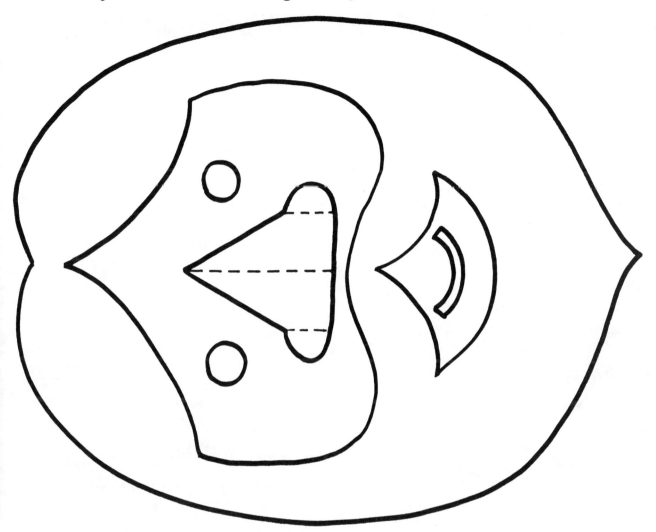

Paper Plate Face Pattern: Moses and The Ten Commandments

Patterns may be used this size or enlarged to fit your needs.

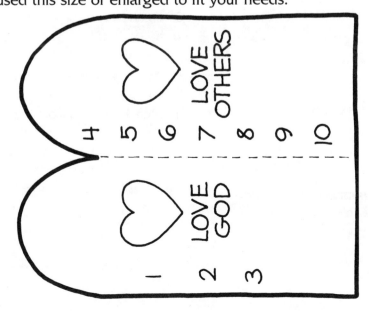

PAPER PLATE FACE

What You Need

Paper plate

Jumbo craft stick

Glue

Markers or crayons

What You Do

1. Use markers to draw the puppet face, hair, and beard on the paper plate.

2. Glue a jumbo craft stick to the back of the paper plate.

3. Hold the puppet as you tell the story.

More to Do

1. Glue on yarn for the hair and beard.

2. Using patterns on page 15, cut facial features from construction paper and glue them to paper plate.

3. Use movable craft eyes.

4. Instead of a craft stick, tape a dowel or paint stick to the back of the puppet.

5. Make adult faces from large paper plates, children's faces from small plates.

6. Use paper plates of varying colors.

7. Make storytelling props with paper plates and construction paper.

Production Possibilities

• Use small paper plate puppets for a small-group presentation or around a classroom table.

• Use large paper plate puppets for medium- to large-group presentations. Stage possibilities include a three-sided or card-table stage.

• Encourage each child to make a paper plate puppet to represent him- or herself to use in a lesson application outside the classroom.

The Lesson Connection

The Ten Commandments: Deuteronomy 5:1–22

Use the illustration shown here as a guide and make a puppet to represent Moses. Fold another plate in half and cut connected tablets of stone along the fold. Write the numbers for the Ten Commandments on the tablets. Glue craft sticks to the back of both puppets. Use the puppets to tell the story of the Ten Commandments.

As an option, make cross and heart puppets from more paper plates. Use the cross to remind children how Jesus died to forgive us our sins because we cannot keep the commandments on our own. Show the heart to remind them that we try to keep the commandments out of love and gratitude for what Jesus did for us.

NAPKIN PUPPET

What You Need

Napkin

Construction paper

Rubber band

Yarn

Fine-tip markers

Scissors

Glue

Craft stick

What You Do

1. Unfold the napkin and roll in each side toward the middle, as shown in step 1.

2. Fold over the napkin, with one side half the length of the other. Fasten about an inch below the top of the fold with a rubber band. See step 2.

3. Insert the craft stick into the folded napkin so the center makes a head. See step 3.

4. Cut a length of yarn and tie it around the puppet to make a belt.

5. Cut an oval from construction paper and draw a face on it. Glue the face to the puppet.

6. Hold the puppet by the stick as you tell the story.

More to Do

1. Use colored napkins.

2. Make puppets from tissue paper of varying colors.

3. Duplicate, color, cut out, and glue on any of the faces suggested at the top of this page to make additional characters.

4. Draw faces on white adhesive circles and stick them to the puppet.

5. Insert the craft stick into a ball of oil-based clay to stand the puppet for a tabletop presentation.

6. Use a plastic spoon instead of a craft stick.

7. Use colored tissue paper fastened to paint sticks to make large puppets.

> ### 👑 Napkin Puppet Patterns: Jesus Raises Lazarus
>
> Pattern may be used this size or enlarged to fit your needs.

Production Possibilities

- Use puppets made from small napkins for small group presentations. Possible stages include a box stage with open bottom; three-sided stage; or stage made from a paper bag, cereal box, or milk carton.

- Use puppets made from large dinner napkins or large sheets of tissue paper in a larger classroom setting.

The Lesson Connection

Jesus Raises Lazarus: John 11:17–44

Make puppets to represent Jesus, Mary, Martha, and Lazarus. Use them to tell the story of how Jesus raised Lazarus from the dead, and how, through His own death and resurrection, He will raise us to eternal life as well.

CRAFT STICK PUPPET

What You Need

Jumbo craft sticks

Fine-tip markers

What You Do

1. Draw a figure on the craft stick, leaving space at the bottom to hold the stick.

2. Hold the puppet and use it to tell a story.

More to Do

1. Cut smaller craft sticks in half and glue them to the back of the large craft stick for arms.

2. Glue on clothes made from felt, fabric, or construction paper.

3. Glue on hair made from frayed yarn or use craft store hair.

4. Stand the craft stick puppets by sticking them into the bottom of a Styrofoam tray turned upside down.

Production Possibilities

- This puppet is quick and easy to make for a small group presentation. You can use it alone or with one of these stages: small box stage with open bottom; three-sided stage; or stage made from a paper plate, envelope, paper bag, cereal box, or milk carton.

- Have each student make a set of puppets as well as a paper plate, envelope, or bag stage to use for telling the story at home.

The Lesson Connection

The Baptism of Jesus: Matthew 3:13–17

Draw Jesus on one craft stick and John the Baptist on another. Draw a dove for the Holy Spirit at the top of a third stick. On a paper plate, draw a cloud at the top with rays of light coming from it. Cut a slit large enough for the craft stick to go under the cloud. Draw the riverbank and River Jordan along a slit across the width of the paper plate. Tell the story of Jesus' Baptism as you slip the Jesus and John puppets in the slit at the river. Then slip the dove puppet through slit under the cloud and tell how God the Father spoke and the Holy Spirit appeared in the form of a dove. Use this as an opportunity to teach that God is Three-in-One: Father, Son, and Holy Spirit.

PAINT STICK PUPPET

What You Need

Paint stick

Markers

What You Do

1. Draw a figure on one end of the paint stick.

2. Hold the paint stick at the bottom as you tell the story.

More to Do

1. Duplicate the robe and face on this page and use them to trace and cut a robe and face from felt, construction paper, or fun foam. Glue to the paint stick.

2. Glue smaller craft sticks to the back for arms.

3. Cut figures from Sunday school leaflets, magazines, or newspapers to glue to the paint stick.

4. Paint figures on the sticks using acrylic paints.

5. Use both sides of the paint stick for "before-and-after" stories about Bible characters.

Production Possibilities

• Use for small to medium-sized groups. Stage possibilities include a three-sided stage; card table stage; or stage made from a paper bag, large mailing envelope, or cereal box.

• Let each child make a paint stick puppet to hold as they do a "round-the-table" play.

The Lesson Connection

Saul Becomes Paul: Acts 9:1–19

Draw an angry Saul on one side of the paint stick and a happy Paul on the other. Use the patterns to make the puppet. Cut two robes and glue them to either side of the stick. First show

> ### Paint Stick Puppet Patterns: Saul
> Pattern may be used this size or enlarged to fit your needs.

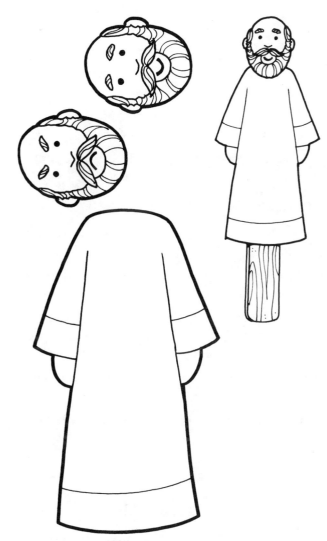

the angry Saul to tell how he harmed the first Christians. Turn the puppet around as you tell the story of Paul's conversion. Tell how Saul changed his name to Paul and went on to proclaim the Gospel to others. Ask who they can tell about Jesus and His love.

WOODEN SPOON PUPPET

What You Need

Wooden spoon   Yarn

Markers   Glue

Scissors

What You Do

1. Use markers to draw a face on a wooden spoon.

2. Cut yarn in small pieces and fray the ends. Glue yarn to the spoon for hair and a beard.

3. Hold the spoon by the handle as you tell the story.

More to Do

1. Omit yarn hair and draw hair and beard with a marker.

2. Glue on doll hair and movable craft eyes (available at most craft and discount stores).

3. Use a needle and thread to gather a strip of fabric or crepe paper and glue it around the base of the spoon to make a robe.

4. Use permanent markers to decorate a plastic jar for a puppet stage.

5. Paint spoon with skin-tone acrylic paint and add facial features.

6. Draw Bible character faces that go from sad to happy on both sides of the spoon.

Production Possibilities

• Use with small to medium-sized classes. Stage possibilities include a box stage with open bottom, three-sided stage, or stage made from a paper bag or cereal box.

• Have children make a puppet to take home to use in telling the story to their family, then hang on the wall as an ongoing reminder of the Bible story.

• Have students make a puppet to represent him- or herself for use in story application.

The Lesson Connection

Mary and Martha: Luke 10:38–42

Make spoon puppets to represent Jesus, Mary, and Martha. Use the puppets to tell the story and then, again, for a story review. Hold up the Mary puppet and ask the children to tell what Mary was doing. Hold up the Martha puppet and ask them to tell what Martha said. Hold up the Jesus puppet and ask what He said. Ask them to think of as many places as possible where they can listen to God's Word, just as Mary listened to Jesus.

STUFFED BAG PUPPET

What You Need

Paper bag   Dowel

Markers   String

Newspaper

What You Do

1. Use markers to draw facial features onto the bag.

2. Stuff bag with newspaper.

3. Place bag over the dowel and use the string to tie it in place.

4. Hold the stick and use the puppet to act out the story.

More to Do

1. Use bags of varying colors and sizes to represent the characters of a Bible story (children and adults, for example).

2. Glue on yarn for hair and movable craft eyes.

3. Use stickers for eyes and mouth.

4. Stuff bags with tissue paper, plastic bags, or paper from a recycling bin.

5. Use construction paper for facial features, hair, and accessories such as crowns.

6. Cut strips of paper and curl them around a pencil or pull the paper, with your thumb on top of it, over a *dull* scissors edge. Glue on the curled strips for 3-D hair.

7. Use permanent markers to draw a puppet face on a plastic bag.

Production Possibilities

· Use puppets made from lunch bags and jumbo craft sticks for small classroom presentations around a table.

· Make puppets from large grocery bags for large group or church presentations. Use a three-sided or card table stage for performing the Bible story.

The Lesson Connection

Josiah Finds God's Word: 2 Kings 22, 23:1–27

Make a stuffed bag puppet to represent Josiah. Have Josiah tell the story of how God's Word was lost, then found again, and read to all the people. Remind the children that God's Word is truth and that through God's Word we learn about His great love-plan: that Jesus died and rose for us.

POP-UP PUPPET

What You Need

Styrofoam cup   Crayons

Permanent markers   Scissors

Craft stick   Glue

Construction paper

What You Do

1. Use permanent markers to draw details on the Styrofoam cup.

2. Draw the pop-up figure on a piece of construction paper. Color it, cut it out, and glue the shape to one end of a craft stick.

3. Poke the stick through the inside bottom of the cup. Push it up when the pop-up is needed as you tell the Bible story.

More to Do

1. Use construction paper, fabric, or felt to add details to the cup.

2. Make the pop-up figure from poster board.

3. Make a head "pop up" by attaching a small Styrofoam ball to a dowel. Decorate the head to look like a face. Poke the dowel through the inside bottom of the cup. Gather a piece of fabric under the head, then glue the opposite edge of the fabric to the inside edge of the cup.

4. Instead of a cup, use a Popsicle push-up, cardboard tube, small cereal box, large cup, or oatmeal box for a pop-up puppet base.

Production Possibilities

• Use small pop-up puppets with a small class.

• Make a pop-up puppet from an oatmeal container to use in front of a large group.

• Have children make a pop-up puppet to use

☼ Pop-up Puppet Pattern: Naaman

Pattern may be used this size or enlarged to fit your needs.

in telling the story at home.

• Adapt this puppet to tell how Jesus healed the paralyzed man who "popped up" from his mat (see Mark 2:1–12).

The Lesson Connection

Naaman Is Healed: 2 Kings 5:1–14

Use permanent markers to draw water around a Styrofoam cup. Photocopy or trace, color, and cut out the Naaman figure shown on this page. Glue the figure to the end of one stick. Punch the bottom of the stick through the bottom of the cup. Have the children count along as you move the stick up and down to show that Naaman bathed in the Jordan seven times. Use this opportunity to teach how the waters of Baptism cleanse us from our sin.

BOTTLE PUPPET

What You Need

Plastic bottle   Markers

Dowel   Scissors

Construction paper   White glue

What You Do

1. The bottle is held upside down for presenting the Bible story.

2. Cut a strip of skin-tone construction paper and glue it around the plastic bottle.

3. Cut a triangle for the nose. Fold it in half. Fold up the corners to make nostrils. Glue the nose to the face. (See 3-D face puppet on page 14 for nose pattern.)

4. Draw eyes and mouth or cut them from construction paper.

5. Cut strips of paper and curl them around a pencil or pull the paper, with your thumb on top of it, over a *dull* scissors edge. Glue on the curled strips for 3-D hair. Cut a construction paper circle to fit to the top of the puppet head and glue in place. If needed, add a construction paper beard.

6. Put a dowel inside the puppet and hold the stick as you tell the story.

More to Do

1. Use acrylics to paint a skin-tone over a clear plastic bottle, then paint facial features.

2. Draw facial features with a permanent marker.

3. Use doll hair (available at craft or discount stores) or frayed yarn for hair and beards and glue it to the bottle.

4. Glue on movable craft eyes.

5. Instead of a dowel, insert the handle of a wooden spoon inside the bottle.

Production Possibilities

· Students can hold small bottle puppets for small-group performances. Small bottle puppets can be used with a small box stage or three-sided stage.

· Use large (2 liter) bottle puppets for large-group performances. Large bottle puppets can be used with a card table stage.

The Lesson Connection

Joshua Leads God's People: Joshua 1–3

Make a puppet to represent Joshua. Have students make 12 bottle puppets to represent the 12 Tribes of Israel. Using the Joshua puppet, tell the story of how God chose him to lead the children of Israel into the Promised Land. Expand the story to teach the children the words of Joshua as found in Joshua 24:15b: "As for me and my household, we will serve the LORD." Invite each child to hold the puppet and recite the verse.

STAND-UP PUPPETS
PLASTIC SPOON PUPPET

What You Need

Plastic spoon

Permanent markers

Styrofoam tray

What You Do

1. Draw a face on the back of a plastic spoon.

2. Stick the spoon handle into the upside-down Styrofoam tray as you tell the story.

More to Do

1. Use plastic spoons in a variety of colors for different characters.

2. Stick a gummed circle to the back of the spoon; use markers to add facial features.

3. Glue on moveable craft eyes.

4. Use plastic forks for another kind of puppet.

5. Place the spoon handle into a ball of oil-based clay to make a tabletop puppet.

Production Possibilities

• Use as a fast, easy way to make a number of puppets for use with a small group sitting at a table or in a circle of chairs.

• Stick spoons through an upside-down Styrofoam bowl or egg carton for an instant stage, or hold them up in a small box stage; three-sided stage; or a stage made from a paper bag, cereal box, or milk carton.

• Let children make a set of plastic spoon puppets to use in telling the story at home.

The Lesson Connection

Jesus Calls Four Fishermen: Matthew 4:18–22

Make spoon puppets for Jesus, James, John, Andrew, and Peter. Stick spoons into an upside down Styrofoam bowl or tray as you tell how Jesus called the four men to be "fishers of men." Explain how fishing for men means sharing the Good News of the Gospel. Share how Jesus calls each one of us to "follow Him" and to be "fishers of men."

CLOTHESPIN PUPPET

What You Need

Clothespin

Pipe cleaner

Fine-tip marker

Felt or fabric

Yarn

Craft glue

Oil-based clay

What You Do

1. Use markers to draw a face on the head of the clothespin.

2. Twist a pipe cleaner around the neck of the clothespin and shape the two ends to form arms and hands.

3. Using the illustration on this page as a guide, make a robe from felt or fabric. Place the robe over the puppet's head and arms. Use yarn to tie a belt around the middle of the clothespin.

4. Glue yarn to the puppet head for hair and a beard.

5. To stand the clothespin, stick it in a ball of oil-based clay.

More to Do

1. Make a head by cutting a square from pantyhose, placing a cotton ball inside, and tying the pantyhose around the clothespin head.

2. If you make the pantyhose head, cut a strip of fabric and tie it around the head with yarn to form a robe.

3. Use other kinds of fabric, tissue paper, or napkins for clothing.

4. Glue on movable craft eyes.

5. Make a set of clothespin puppets to use for a variety of lessons.

Production Possibilities

- Use for small classroom presentations with a tabletop or box stage.

- Have children make their own clothespin puppets to take home and tell the story to others.

The Lesson Connection

The Forgiving Father: Luke 15:11–32

Make puppets to represent the father and two sons. Make a table top stage: cut a strip of shelf paper or poster board, and use crayons to draw a house at one end and a road leading to a pigpen at the other end. Move the puppets on the stage as you tell the story of the father's forgiving love for his son. Expand the story to teach about the forgiving love of God our Father. Tell how God welcomes us back as we turn away from sin and look to Him for forgiveness and strength.

STYROFOAM CUP PUPPET

What You Need

Styrofoam cup

Permanent markers

What You Do

1. Turn the cup upside down. Draw a circle toward the top of the cup for a head. Add a face, hair, and optional beard.

2. Draw an arm on each side of the puppet. Add a robe and belt if you wish.

3. Move the figure on the table as you tell the Bible story.

More to Do

1. Use construction paper to glue on a face and clothes. Add paper arms—either two separate arms or a strip of paper with hands on each end encircling the figure.

2. Use cups of varying sizes for different characters.

3. Glue a stick inside the cup to change it into a stick puppet.

4. Instead of a face and body, draw just a face on the puppet.

5. Place your hand inside the cup to use it as a hand puppet.

6. Have students make one puppet a week during Advent to take home for a nativity set.

7. Omit the oval face and draw facial features above the neckline.

Production Possibilities

- Use small cups for small-group teaching situations. Move the puppets over a tabletop stage or box stage with open top. Have each child hold a puppet for an around-the-table presentation.

- Use larger cups for presentations to bigger groups.

- Make puppets from large ice cream or deli containers for presentation to a larger group.

The Lesson Connection

The Woman at the Well: John 4:1–26

Draw a figure to represent Jesus on one cup and the woman at the well on another. As an option, cut and glue on a construction paper robe and head, using the patterns on page 27. Draw stones on a third cup to make a well. Use the puppets to tell this story of Jesus' love and forgiveness. Remind them that His love and forgiveness are for everyone—no matter who we are, where we live, what we look like, or what we have done.

Styrofoam Cup Puppet Patterns: Jesus and the Woman

Patterns may be used this size or enlarged to fit your needs.

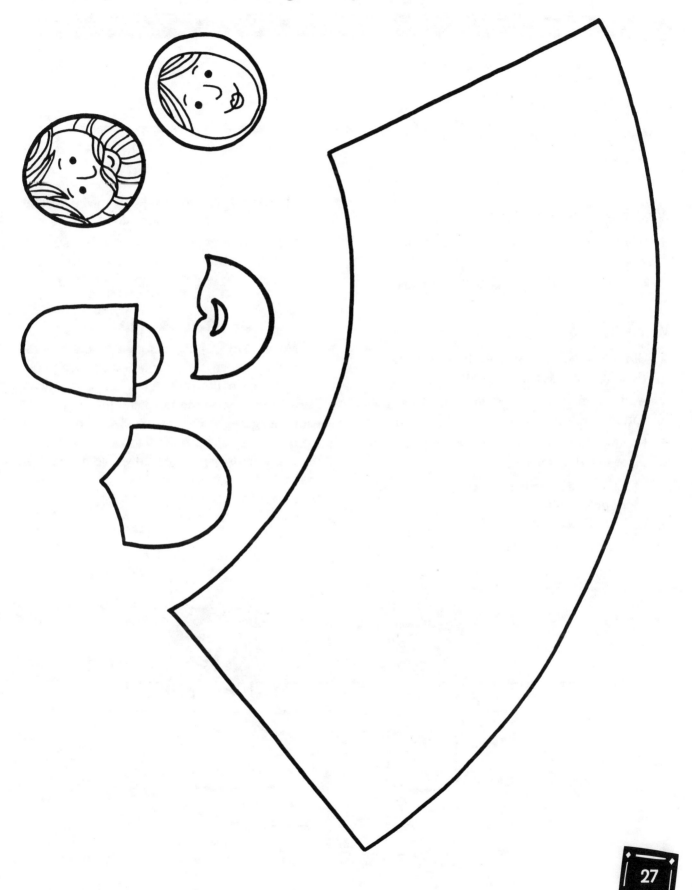

WOODEN CRAFT FIGURE PUPPET

What You Need

Wooden craft figure

Markers

What You Do

1. Use markers to draw a face and body on the wooden figure.

2. Move the figure on a table as you tell the story.

More to Do

1. Use felt or fabric to add a robe to the figure. Tie a belt with a piece of yarn.

2. Add hair made from craft hair, frayed yarn, or cotton.

3. Have children decorate wooden figures to place in a diorama.

4. Make a set of wooden figures to use in classroom presentations.

5. Use different sizes of wooden figures to depict children and adults.

6. Paint figure with acrylics.

7. Draw a scene on a strip of shelf paper or poster board for a tabletop stage.

Production Possibilities

· Use with a tabletop stage or small box stage for a small group presentation.

· Have children make puppets and a stage to take home and use to tell the story to others.

The Lesson Connection

The Good Samaritan: Luke 10:25–37

Make a wooden figure for each person in the story. On a piece of poster board or shelf paper, draw the road between Jerusalem and Jericho. Place the paper on the table and follow the road with the figures as you tell Jesus' story of how we are to love and help our neighbor. Make a list of the many kinds of people God would have us call "neighbor." Tell the children that when God sent Jesus as our Savior, He made Himself our neighbor.

PLASTIC CUP PUPPET

What You Need

Small plastic cup

Permanent markers

What You Do

1. Turn the cup upside down.
2. Use the markers to draw a face on the cup. Add hair and, if needed, a beard.
3. Move the cup as you tell the story.

More to Do

1. Instead of just a face, draw the whole puppet body on the cup.
2. Glue a craft stick inside the cup to make a stick puppet.
3. To make an angel, glue a half circle of white lace or half of a paper doily to the back of the puppet. Use a glitter pen to add features.

Production Possibilities

These puppets provide a quick way to create a crowd of puppet people to use in a small group production. Use directly on a classroom table, on a tabletop stage, or in a small box stage with open bottom.

Have each child make a puppet for use in an around-the-table presentation.

The Lesson Connection

Jesus Heals Ten Lepers: Luke 17:11–19

Draw a face to represent Jesus on one cup. Draw faces on ten other cups to represent the lepers. Have the children help you move the ten leper puppets away when Jesus heals them. Then return one cup to represent the man who came back to thank Jesus for what He did. Make a list of the many things we can thank Jesus for. Remember to include the most important—the forgiveness and eternal life that is ours through His death and resurrection.

OATMEAL BOX PUPPET

What You Need

Oatmeal box Markers or crayons

Construction paper Glue

Scissors

What You Do

1. Turn the oatmeal box upside down.

2. Cut a strip of paper and glue it around the top third or fourth of the box to make the puppet head. Cut a different color of paper to glue around the rest of the box. Cut a strip to fit around the head for a headdress. Glue on the strips.

3. Cut eyes, nose, and beard to glue onto the face.

4. Cut a strip of paper for each arm. Cut and glue a hand to the end of each piece. Glue the arms to the body.

5. Place your hand in the oatmeal box to move the puppet.

More to Do

1. Use felt or fabric instead of construction paper.

2. Use markers to add details.

3. Tie yarn around the headdress.

4. Use different sizes of oatmeal boxes.

5. Tape dowels inside the puppets for use as stick puppets.

Production Possibilities

· Have each child hold a puppet for an around-the-table story.

· Move the puppets on a tabletop stage as you tell the story.

· Large puppets can be used on a table at the front of the congregation or other large group to tell the Christmas story, then left for a manger scene in the fellowship area.

The Lesson Connection

The Wise Men: Matthew 2:1–12

Make three Wise Men puppets and add a gift for each to hold. Make puppets to represent Herod and his advisors and to represent Joseph, Mary, and baby Jesus. Move the Wise Men across the table on their way to find their newborn King. Explain that the Wise Men came from far away. Tell how this Bible story teaches that Jesus came to be Messiah and King for all people everywhere.

Oatmeal Box Puppet Patterns: Wise Men

Patterns may be used this size or enlarged to fit your needs.

STAND-UP PAPER PUPPET

What You Need

Paper

Markers

Scissors

Glue

What You Do

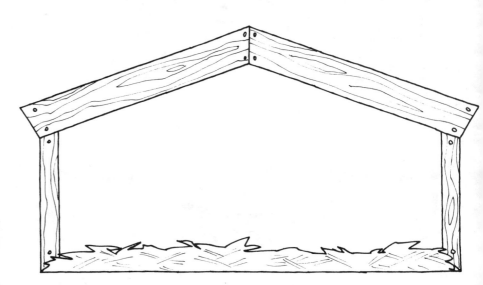

1. Draw a figure onto the paper using the patterns on the next page.

2. Cut a strip of paper. Glue the strip together to form a loop and glue the figure to it.

3. Move the figure on a flat surface as you tell the story.

More to Do

1. Make figures from construction paper or index cards.

2. Use strip loops and glue on figures cut from old Sunday school leaflets, magazines, or other picture sources.

3. Laminate figures for more durability.

4. Enlarge figures and glue small tubes or boxes behind them to stand them up.

Production Possibilities

· Small figures are suitable for tabletop presentations or for use with a small box stage with open top.

· Larger figures backed with tubes or boxes can be used for a large group presentation.

· Have children make puppets and stage from a shoebox to take home.

The Lesson Connection

The Christmas Story: Luke 2:1–20

Make a set of figures to illustrate the story of Jesus' birth. Glue paper loops behind each one. Use the pattern shown for a stable, or make a stable from a shoebox. As a review, show each figure and ask how it is important to the story. Remind children that they are important to Jesus, who came as Savior for each and every one.

Stand-up Paper Puppet Patterns: The Christmas Story

Patterns may be used this size or enlarged to fit your needs.

Fold at the dotted line so characters apear to be kneeling.

INDEX CARD PUPPET

What You Need

Index card

Fine-tip markers

Scissors

What You Do

1. Fold the index card in half. Trace the pattern onto the index card, along the fold.

2. Cut along the fold to make a symmetrical puppet.

3. Use fine-tip markers to add detail.

4. Move the puppet as you tell the story.

More to Do

1. Use the pattern to trace and cut puppets from colored or marbled index paper.

2. Cut puppets from colored index cards. Stick on gummed circles or glue on paper ovals for faces. Use fine-tip markers to add facial and clothing details.

3. Cut puppets from construction paper or other heavyweight paper.

4. Glue on a craft stick to make a stick puppet.

5. Cut shapes ahead of time and have children color and assemble them as a lesson-related activity.

6. Use crayons or markers to color puppets cut from white paper.

Production Possibilities

· These are fast, easily made puppets that can be used with small classes on a tabletop or small box stage.

· Have children make a set of puppets to take home.

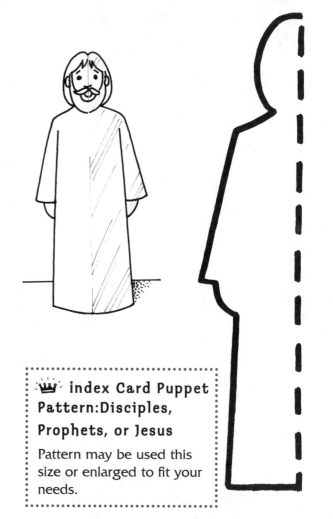

index Card Puppet Pattern: Disciples, Prophets, or Jesus

Pattern may be used this size or enlarged to fit your needs.

The Lesson Connection

The Transfiguration: Matthew 17:1–13

Make index-card puppets to represent Jesus, Peter, James, John, Elijah, and Moses. Use them to tell how Jesus went with Peter, James, and John to the top of a mountain. Tell how the three disciples saw the appearance of Jesus change to show His glory. Add Elijah and Moses. Remind the children that God the Father spoke—just as He did at Jesus' Baptism. Remind them that God still speaks to us in His Word.

FILM CANISTER PUPPET

What You Need

35mm film canister   Glue

Construction paper   Scissors

Fine-tip markers

What You Do

1. Cut a strip of skin-tone construction paper. Glue it around the top third or fourth of the film canister.

2. Cut a different color of construction paper to fit the rest of the canister. Glue it around the bottom of the canister.

3. Make arms by cutting a strip of paper to fit around the canister. Cut two hands and glue one to the end of each arm. Glue arms in place so each end stands out from the side of the figure.

4. Use markers to draw facial features, hair, and a beard, if needed.

5. Move the puppet on the table as you tell the story.

More to Do

1. Use permanent markers to draw faces or complete figures directly onto different colored film canisters (such as white or gray).

2. Cover the canister with felt, fabric, or other material.

3. Use craft hair or yarn and glue on hair and a beard.

4. Glue or tape a craft stick inside the canister to make a stick puppet.

5. Use film canisters as finger puppets.

6. Use plastic frosting canisters to make bigger puppets.

7. Put rice inside the canister. Glue on the lid with a hot glue gun. Shake the canister to make the puppet sing a song of praise.

Production Possibilities

- Use for small group presentations either on a tabletop or small box theater with open top.

- Have each child make a "shaker puppet" to use in singing songs of praise as part of a lesson application.

The Lesson Connection

Miriam Sings a Song of Joy: Exodus 15:19–21

Make a puppet to represent Miriam. Add a construction paper tambourine to her hand. Add rice to the inside of the canister and glue on the lid. Ask the children to join you in Miriam's song of joy to the melody "Row, Row, Row Your Boat."

Sing, sing, unto the Lord,
For He does marvelous things!
The Lord is my strength, the Lord is my
    song;
He is my salvation.

CARDBOARD TUBE PUPPET

What You Need

Cardboard tube   Scissors

Construction paper   Glue

Markers

What You Do

1. Using the patterns on the next page, cut a skin-tone strip of paper around the top of the tube and glue it in place. Draw eyes, a nose, and a mouth.

2. Cut construction paper hair to fit onto the tube. Glue it in place.

3. Cut a strip of colored construction paper to fit around the rest of the tube and glue it on.

4. Cut two arms for your tube. Cut and glue a hand to each arm. Then glue each arm to the puppet.

5. Move the puppet around on a tabletop stage as you tell the story.

More to Do

1. Glue a craft stick to the top of the tube to enable you to move the puppet from the top on a table or in a box stage.

2. Glue a craft stick to the bottom of the tube to use it as a stick puppet.

3. Use felt, wallpaper, or cloth instead of construction paper.

4. Glue paper around the tube and let children draw on details with markers.

5. Make a set of cardboard tube puppets to use with a variety of lessons.

Production Possibilities

- Use with a tabletop or box stage for a small to medium-sized classroom presentation.

- Have children make several puppets and a box theater to take home.

The Lesson Connection

Joseph and His Brothers: Genesis 37:2–36, 42–45

Use rainbow-striped wrapping paper or wallpaper for Joseph's coat. Cut construction paper stones to glue on a Styrofoam cup to make a well. Use the puppets to tell the story of Joseph being sold into Egypt and how he later forgave his brothers. Expand this into a discussion of how Jesus forgives our sins and helps us forgive others too.

Cardboard Tube Puppet Pattern: Joseph

Patterns may be used this size or enlarged to fit your needs.

PAPER TUBE PUPPET

What You Need

Paper

Scissors

Markers or crayons

Glue

What You Do

1. Cut strips of paper.

2. Draw a figure on the center of the strip. Use the pattern shown here page as a guide.

3. Glue the ends of the strip together.

4. Stand the puppet and use it to tell a story.

More to Do

1. Glue figures from old Sunday school lesson leaflets or magazines to the strip of paper.

2. Glue stickers to shorter strips of paper and use them as mini-puppets or finger puppets.

Production Possibilities

• Use small tubes with small group tabletop presentations or with a small box stage with open top.

• Large tube puppets can be used with large groups and for a church sanctuary production.

The Lesson Connection

Paul's Missionary Journeys: Acts 13–28

Make a tube puppet to represent Paul. Have children make several more tube puppets to represent the people who heard Paul preach to them about Jesus. Draw a simple map of the countries Paul visited on a piece of poster board for a table-

Paper Tube Puppet: Paul

Pattern may be used this size or enlarged to fit your needs

top stage. Put the poster board on the table and place the puppets at the various places Paul visited. Move Paul over the map as you review the places he went to tell people of Jesus' saving love. Place puppets at the cities to whom Paul's epistles were addressed and explain that the epistles are letters Paul wrote to the new Christians.

LUNCH BAG PUPPET

What You Need

Lunch bag

Yarn

Markers or crayons

Newspaper

What You Do

1. Using the illustration as a guide, draw a face, hair, and beard on the top part of the lunch bag.

2. Draw arms and clothing on the bottom of the bag.

3. Stuff the bag to the neckline with wadded newspaper. Tie the bag at the neckline with a piece of yarn.

4. Move the puppet on a table as you tell the story.

More to Do

1. Glue on construction paper to make the head and robe.

2. Tie off the neck with a rubber band.

3. Make puppets from a variety of bag sizes and colors to represent children and adults.

4. Cut a hole in the bottom of the bag and put a dowel into the bag to use it as a stick puppet.

Production Possibilities

· Use puppets made from lunch bags on a tabletop stage for a small group.

· For a large-group presentation, make puppets from large grocery bags and move them on a tabletop at the front of the room.

The Lesson Connection

Simeon and Anna: Luke 2:21–38

Draw the face of an old man to represent Simeon onto a lunch bag, and the face of an old woman representing Anna onto another bag. Have each puppet tell how they praised God when Mary and Joseph brought the infant Jesus to the temple. Sing the following song to the melody "Mary Had a Little Lamb" to help children learn the story.

Let me, Lord, now go in peace,
Go in peace, go in peace;
Your salvation, I have seen—
A light for all the world.

STAND-UP BOTTLE PUPPET

What You Need

Plastic bottle	Pipe cleaner
Styrofoam ball	Glue
Yarn	Scissors
Permanent marker	Uncooked rice or dried beans
Fabric	

What You Do

1. Stand the plastic bottle.

2. Wrap the pipe cleaner around the neck and bend the ends to form a hand on each arm.

3. Lay the bottle on a piece of fabric and draw a robe shape onto the fabric. Cut out the robe. Glue the robe around the arms and body of the puppet.

4. Put enough rice or dried beans in the bottle to add enough weight for it to stand steadily.

5. Draw a face onto the Styrofoam ball.

6. Glue on yarn for hair.

7. Stick the Styrofoam ball onto the bottle. Glue it in place.

8. Move the bottle around on a table as you tell the story.

More to Do

1. Use craft store hair for the puppet. Or make hair by wrapping yarn around an index card, tying off one end, and cutting apart the other end.

2. Consider a variety of fabrics and other materials for clothing: burlap, felt, wrapping paper. Or use ready-made doll clothes.

3. Paint the face with tempera or acrylic paint.

4. Glue on craft-store movable eyes for the face. Glue on a nose and mouth cut from felt.

5. Use different sizes of plastic bottles for different sizes of puppet people.

6. Use the puppet head alone as a finger puppet. Gather a piece of fabric or paper napkin around your finger for the puppet's robe.

7. If the bottle shape is not indented at the top, omit the Styrofoam ball and with permanent markers draw the puppet face directly on the top section of the bottle.

Production Possibilities

- For small to medium classes, use small bottles on a tabletop stage or box stage with open top.

- Use large bottles for large group presentations.

The Lesson Connection

Queen Esther: The Book of Esther

Make a puppet to represent Queen Esther. Add a crown made from gold wrapping paper or from a strand of sequins. Use alone to tell the story or make additional puppets to act out the story of God's faithfulness to His people. Remind the children that God's faithfulness never fails.

BALLOON PUPPET

What You Need

Balloon
Permanent markers
Tape
Construction paper
Scissors

What You Do

1. Blow up balloon and knot the end.

2. Use markers to draw a face on the balloon.

3. Cut out construction paper feet for a base.

4. Tape the knotted end of the balloon to the base.

5. Move the balloon on a surface as you tell a story.

More to Do

1. Cut construction paper features to glue to the balloon.

2. Make a marionette by adding a string tied to the balloon's knot.

3. Add accordion-fold strips of paper to represent arms and legs.

4. Draw a face on a round balloon or a face and body on a longer balloon.

5. Use for both people and animals.

6. Use a balloon pump, available at craft stores and party shops, to blow up large numbers of balloons.

7. To make a papier-mâché balloon puppet, cover the balloon with strips of newspaper dipped into flour paste or wallpaper paste. Finish with a layer of white paper and let dry. Use tempera paint to add details. Insert a stick into a hole cut at the bottom of the papier-mâché balloon to make it into a stick puppet.

8. Books on twisting long balloons into different shapes are available in book, craft, and party stores. Make shapes to use as one-time class-room puppets or in making papier-mâché puppets.

9. Make a base by pulling the balloon knot through the center hole of a fast-food beverage lid.

Production Possibilities

· Good for a small group presentation in which children place the balloon puppet on a table in front of them.

· Use on a table in front of a large classroom.

The Lesson Connection

Adam Names the Animals: Genesis 2:19–20

Have each child make a balloon and decorate it to represent an animal. Make one balloon to represent Adam. Have the children take turns holding up their animal for Adam to name as you tell the story from the Bible.

FINGER PUPPETS

FINGERTIP PUPPET

What You Need

Fingers, yours or children's

Water-based, fine-tip markers

Towel

Soap

Water

What You Do

1. Draw faces on the tips of your fingers.

2. Hold up your fingers as you tell the story.

3. Have the towel, soap, and water ready for removing faces when the presentation is done.

More to Do

1. Draw a face on one finger of each child in the class so everyone can take part in telling a story.

2. Draw contemporary faces to use in a classroom lesson application.

3. Instead of drawing on your fingertips, cut a strip of paper, draw a face on it, then tape or glue it around your finger.

4. Gather a strip of material to tie onto your finger under the fingertip puppet.

5. Draw a face onto bandages wrapped around fingertips.

Production Possibilities

• Use for a small-group presentation using a stage made from a paper plate, envelope, paper bag, cereal box, or milk carton.

The Lesson Connection

Jairus's Daughter: Matthew 9:18–25

Cut the top and bottom from a small milk carton. Wash the inside so no milk residue remains. Cover the sides with construction paper. Draw a face to represent Jesus on your index finger; draw a face to represent the little girl on your thumb. As you tell how Jesus raised the little girl, move up your thumb. Sing this song using the melody for "Mary Had a Little Lamb."

"Little girl, get up now,
Get up now, get up now.
Little girl, get up now,"
Said Jesus to the girl.

The little girl got up right then,
Up right then, up right then;
The little girl got up right then,
She was alive once more.

SELF-ADHESIVE CIRCLE PUPPET

What You Need

Self-adhesive circles

Fine-tip markers

What You Do

1. Draw faces on the self-adhesive circles.

2. Stick the circles to your fingers and tell the story.

More to Do

1. Have each child draw a face or set of faces to put on their fingers for a story review.

2. Use adhesive circles in a variety of colors.

3. Stick circles on craft sticks or glove fingers.

Production Possibilities

· Use with a small group presentation. Use with a stage made from a paper plate, envelope, paper bag, cereal box, or milk carton.

The Lesson Connection

Through the Red Sea: Exodus 13:17–14:31

Follow the directions on page 7 to make a long, open-ended cereal box stage. Cut wavy strips of construction paper to glue to the sides of the box. Draw faces on self-adhesive circles and put them on the fingers of one hand. Let your thumb be Moses. Move them through the box opening as you tell the story of how Moses led the Israelites through the Red Sea. Sing this song using the melody "In a Cabin in the Woods."

Long ago the Israelites
Saw a great and glorious sight;
As a path dry as could be
Led through the Red Sea.

Through the water they all crossed;
Not a single soul was lost;
God's great power saved the day.
And sent them on their way.

CIRCLE-FACE FINGER PUPPET

What You Need

Paper

Fine-tip markers

Scissors

Glue

Pencil

What You Do

1. Draw a rectangle long enough to fit around your finger. In the center of the rectangle, draw a circle.

2. Use markers to draw a face and hair in the circle.

3. Cut out the puppet. Size the strip of paper to your finger and glue it together.

4. Put the circle puppet on your finger as you tell a story.

More to Do

1. Trace around round objects of varying sizes, such as coins, to make puppet faces in different sizes.

2. Use crayons or colored pencils to draw puppet faces.

3. Have children make a set of circle finger puppets to take home.

4. Glue circle faces to craft sticks to make stick puppets.

Production Possibilities

• Use for small group presentations with a small box stage with open bottom; three-sided stage; or stage made from a paper bag, cereal box, or milk carton.

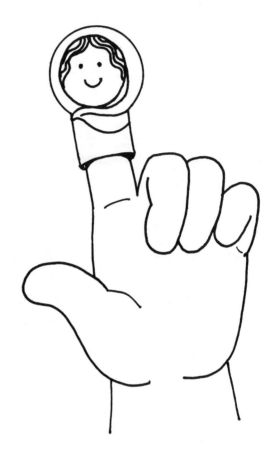

• Have each class member make a puppet to use for an around-the-table story presentation.

The Lesson Connection

Rebekah and Isaac: Genesis 24

Make three puppets to represent Rebekah, Isaac, and Abraham's servant. Start out with only Abraham's servant, then add Rebekah and Isaac as the story continues. Remind the children that God was with Abraham's servant as he went to find a wife for Isaac, and that He is with each of us as we go about, doing our daily tasks.

Circle Face Finger Puppet Patterns: Rebekah and Isaac

Patterns may be used this size or enlarged to fit your needs.

Tube Finger Puppet Patterns: Jesus Feeds 5,000 People

Patterns may be used this size or enlarged to fit your needs.

TUBE FINGER PUPPET

What You Need

Paper

Markers

Scissors

Glue

What You Do

1. Cut strips of paper, about 1½ inches tall, to fit around your finger.

2. Using the patterns and samples shown on page 45, draw a figure or face on the paper.

3. Size the paper to your finger and glue it to make a tube.

4. Put the tube on your finger and use it to tell a story.

More to Do

1. Use crayons or colored pencils to draw the puppet figure.

2. Make the puppet from construction paper and use markers to draw the figure.

3. Give students precut paper strips as they come to class. Have them draw puppet figures as you tell the Bible story. Use the puppets they make for a classroom presentation to review the Bible story.

4. Glue a drinking straw or craft stick inside the tube to turn it into a stick puppet.

5. Decorate a cereal box and set the puppets inside for a diorama.

6. Instead of wearing tube puppets on your fingers, use them for a tabletop or small stage presentation.

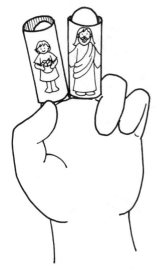

7. Make tube finger puppets from felt or other material.

Production Possibilities

- Use these small puppets for small group presentations. Use a small box stage or small three-sided stage, or use a stage made from a paper bag, cereal box, or milk carton.

- Have class members make a set of puppets and a stage to take home for telling the story to others.

- Make large tube puppets from poster board to use in front of a large classroom or in church.

The Lesson Connection

Jesus Feeds 5,000 People: John 6:1–14

Make puppets to represent Jesus, the boy with five loaves and two fishes, and a disciple. Have children make additional puppets to represent the crowd. Have the children hold their puppets on their fingers while you tell the story. Remind the children that Jesus performed a miracle in this story and that all of Jesus' miracles demonstrate that He is truly the Son of God.

WALKING PUPPET

What You Need

Heavyweight paper

Fine-tip markers

Scissors

What You Do

1. Using the patterns shown here, draw a figure wearing a robe. Use a shorter robe for a figure that will show a lot of action.

2. Cut two holes big enough to put your fingers through at the bottom of the robe. (Your fingers are the puppet's legs.)

3. Place a finger in each hole and "walk" your puppet as you tell a story.

More to Do

1. Use crayons or colored pencils instead of markers.

2. Cut out an outline of a figure to give to each child in the class. Have them draw in the figure for use during the lesson.

3. Laminate puppets for durability.

4. Make puppet from construction paper, an index card, or poster board.

Production Possibilities

• These puppets are best used for small-group presentations on a tabletop stage.

• Have children make their own puppet to use in telling the story at home.

The Lesson Connection

Peter and John Heal a Crippled Man: Acts 3:1–10

Draw two figures with long robes to represent Peter and John. Draw a figure wearing a shorter robe for the crippled man. Have the crippled man "leap for joy" at the point when he is healed. Explain to the children that the power to heal did not belong to Peter and John, but to Jesus. Remind them that Peter said, "In the name of Jesus … walk" (Acts 3:6).

·ᘜ·Walking Puppet Patterns: Disciples and Crippled Man

Patterns may be used this size or enlarged to fit your needs.

PRAYING HANDS PUPPET

What You Need

Heavyweight paper

Fine-tip markers

Scissors

What You Do

1. Using the pattern shown, draw a figure from the waist up.

2. Cut a finger hole at each shoulder.

3. Place your finger and thumb in the holes and use them as you tell the story.

More to Do

1. Use crayons or colored pencils instead of markers.

2. Cut out an outline of a figure to give to each child to color in as him- or herself for a lesson application.

3. Laminate puppets for durability.

4. Cut the puppet from construction paper, index card, or poster board.

5. Use for Bible stories in which arm movements are important to illustrate someone praying or helping someone else.

6. Make a full-body shape with armholes.

Production Possibilities

• Use the finger puppet for a small group presentation around a classroom table.

• For a large-group presentation, draw a large figure on a piece of poster board. Cut both eye and arm holes. Slip your arms through the armholes to act out the story.

The Lesson Connection

The Lord's Prayer: Matthew 6:9–13

Draw a puppet to represent Jesus. Fold Jesus' hands as He teaches His disciples the Lord's Prayer. Trace an outline of the puppet to give to each child. Have them make the puppet to represent themselves, then use it show how they can pray. Use this opportunity to teach the Lord's Prayer and to remind the children that God hears the prayers of all His people. Discuss the many times and places where we can pray.

Praying Hands Puppet Pattern: Jesus and His Disciples

Pattern may be used this size or enlarged to fit your needs.

GLOVE FINGERTIP PUPPET

What You Need

Gardening glove   Scissors

Yarn   Glue

Fine-tip markers

What You Do

1. Cut off the tip of a gardening glove finger.

2. Use markers to draw on facial features.

3. Glue on yarn for hair and, if needed, a beard.

4. Place the puppet on your finger and use it as you tell a story.

More to Do

1. Glue or sew on felt facial features, craft hair, and other details.

2. Use Velcro to change faces.

3. Use a glove fingertip as a pattern and sew your own puppet.

4. Cut glove fingers short for just a puppet face or long for a puppet's whole body.

5. Cut fingers from a rubber glove and draw on features with a permanent marker.

Production Possibilities

- Use for small group presentations with a stage made from a paper plate, paper bag, cereal box, or milk carton.

- Pass the glove fingertip puppet around to have children take turns telling the story in their own words.

- Have children make glove fingertip puppets to take home for sharing Bible stories with their family.

The Lesson Connection

Daniel in the Lion's Den: Daniel 6:1–28

Cut fingertips from a gardening glove. Make puppets for Daniel, the angel of the Lord, and three lions. Use small pieces of yarn to make manes for the lions and hair for Daniel and the angel. Use markers or felt for facial details. Make an open-ended cereal box stage. Cover the side with gray construction paper and draw rocks. Tell the story of how God sent the angel to keep Daniel safe in the lion's den. Remind them that God's love and protection are with us wherever we go.

HAND PUPPETS
LUNCH BAG HAND PUPPET

What You Need

Paper lunch bag

Markers

What You Do

1. Position the paper bag with the fold in front, facing you.

2. Draw the mouth with the top lip above the fold and the bottom lip below the fold.

3. Draw eyes and a nose.

4. Draw a curved line below the mouth for a chin or add a moustache and beard.

5. Place your hand inside the puppet and move the flap to open and close the puppet mouth as it "talks."

More to Do

1. Glue on a construction paper face. Cut a top and bottom lip to glue onto the face above and below the flap. Add circle eyes. Glue on strips of construction paper or yarn for hair. Glue a strip of paper below the face for the figure's robe.

2. Use wrapping paper or fabric for the figure's robe.

3. Adapt the patterns provided on the following page to individual puppet needs.

Production Possibilities

• Use for small or medium classes. Let each child around a table hold a puppet, or use puppets with a three-sided or card table stage or inside a box stage open at the bottom.

• Have children make a puppet to use at home to tell the story.

• Have children make a puppet to represent themselves to use as a lesson application.

The Lesson Connection

Jesus Heals Peter's Mother-in-Law: Mark 1:29–31

Make three puppets to represent Jesus, Peter, and Peter's mother-in-law. Use them to tell how Jesus healed the sick woman. Or make one puppet to represent Peter's mother-in-law and have her tell how Jesus healed her. Lead the children in prayer, thanking Jesus for healing us according to His will.

Lunch Bag Hand Puppet Patterns: Jesus Heals Peter's Mother-in-Law

Enlarge patterns to fit your needs.

STUFFED ANIMAL PUPPET

What You Need

Stuffed animal

Scissors

What You Do

1. Use a stuffed animal large enough for your hand to fit inside.

2. Cut a hole in the back of the toy and remove enough stuffing so you can slip your hand inside.

3. Place your hand inside the puppet and move it as you tell your story.

More to Do

1. Use felt or fabric to add other details to your puppet.

2. Purchase a variety of stuffed animals at a thrift store or garage sale to use as puppets for storytelling and lesson applications.

Production Possibilities

- Depending upon its size, stuffed animal puppets can be used for teaching both large and small groups. Use them with a three-sided or card table stage, or hold them as you talk.

- Use a stuffed animal puppet during worship for children's talks, or use them for lesson applications in the classroom.

The Lesson Connection

The Lost Lamb: Matthew 18:10–14

Use a stuffed lamb to make a puppet and tell—from the lamb's perspective—Jesus' parable of the lost lamb. Sing the following song using the melody "Oh, Where, Oh, Where Has My Little Dog Gone."

Oh, where, oh, where has the little lamb gone?
Oh, where, oh, where can he be?
The day is gone, and he's far from home,
Oh, where, oh, where can he be?

The Shepherd searches for His lost lamb.
Until He finds him at last,
Then picks the lamb up in kind, gentle hands
And carries the lamb home at last.

PAPER PLATE HAND PUPPET

What You Need

Two paper plates

Glue

Markers

What You Do

1. Draw a face on the outside of one paper plate.

2. Cut the second paper plate in half.

3. Glue the second plate to the back of the first plate.

4. Fit your hand inside the puppet and move it as you tell a story.

More to Do

1. Cut construction paper details and glue to your puppet.

2. Glue on yarn for the puppet's hair. Add moveable eyes.

3. Use large paper plates to represent adults and small paper plates to represent children.

4. Staple or tape the puppet together for more stability.

Production Possibilities

· Use small puppets only with small groups. Use large paper plates with both small and large classes.

· Use puppet with a three-sided or card table stage.

· Let each child make a puppet to hold for an around-the-table presentation.

The Lesson Connection

Adam and Eve: Genesis 3

Make one puppet to represent Adam and another to represent Eve. Have them tell the story of their fall into sin and the promise of a Savior. Take this opportunity to remind the children that God's promise of a Savior was fulfilled in Jesus Christ. Explain that Jesus came as both God and man to live a perfect life and to take our sins to the cross. Because of Jesus, we are forgiven and free.

PAPER PLATE CONE PUPPET

What You Need

Paper plate

Markers

Scissors

Glue

What You Do

1. Cut a paper plate in half.

2. Draw a circle face, arms, and other features on the paper plate.

3. Glue the sides of the half circle together, adjusting the width to fit your hand.

4. Place your hand inside the cone and move it as a puppet.

More to Do

1. Make your cone puppet from different colors of paper plates or half circles cut from construction paper.

2. Glue on yarn or craft store doll hair.

3. Add construction paper arms and clothes.

4. Use tape instead of glue to form the cone.

Production Possibilities

- Cone puppets can be used with both small and medium groups.

- Use the puppets on a tabletop stage or from behind a three-sided stage, card table stage, or stage open at the bottom.

The Lesson Connection

An Angel Appears to Mary: Luke 1:26–38

Make two cone puppets, one for Mary and one for the angel. Cut a half circle from construction paper or a paper doily and glue it behind the angel to make wings. Have each child make a set of puppets to take home to tell the story and use for an Advent decoration. Use the puppet to lead the children in their own song of praise to God using the melody "Jimmy Crack Corn."

I will praise my God today;
I will praise my God today;
I will praise my God today—
My Savior is my joy!

I will praise my God today;
I will praise my God today;
I will praise my God today—
For all He does for me!

FELT HAND PUPPET

What You Need

Felt	Scissors
Yarn	Marker
Craft glue	Chalk

What You Do

1. Using the illustration on this page as a guide, draw a chalk outline of your hand on a piece of felt. Draw the outline large enough to fit over your hand after you have glued the edges of the felt together.

2. Glue the sides of the puppet together.

3. Cut a flesh-toned felt oval and glue it on for a face.

4. Cut a mouth and eyes from felt and glue them to the puppet's face.

5. Glue on yarn for hair and beard, if needed.

6. Put your hand inside the puppet and use it to tell a story.

More to Do

1. Draw in facial features with fine-tip markers.

2. Glue on movable craft eyes.

3. Glue on hair cut from felt, or use craft hair.

4. Sew around the edges of the puppet.

5. Use another kind of fabric for the puppet body.

6. Use pinking shears to cut out the puppet shape.

Production Possibilities

• Use for both small and medium groups with a box stage open at the bottom, three-sided stage, or card table stage.

• Have children make a puppet to represent themselves to use for story applications.

The Lesson Connection

Dorcas Helps Others: Acts 9:36–42

Make a puppet to represent Dorcas. Let her tell the story of how Peter raised her from the dead and how she used her life to tell others about Jesus. Discuss how the Bible tells us that Dorcas did many kind things to help the poor. Remind the children that God can use our acts of kindness to demonstrate His love to those around us.

OTHER PUPPETS

SHADOW PUPPET

What You Need

Black paper

Pencil

Scissors

Overhead projector

Screen or white wall

What You Do

1. Draw figures on a piece of paper and cut them out.

2. Place the figures on an overhead projector.

3. Move the figures as you tell the story.

More to Do

1. Cut figures from old Sunday school lesson leaflets or magazines to use as shadow puppets.

2. Place the figures on a thin plastic strip for moving them on the overhead screen.

3. Make puppets yourself or have each child draw and cut out a figure.

4. Make shadow props to add to the projected scene.

Production Possibilities

· The projected scene can be used with groups of any size.

The Lesson Connection

Good Friday: Luke 23:26–56

Duplicate and cut out the patterns on the following page. Trace them onto black paper to make three crosses, a hill, a tomb, and a stone. Use the crosses and hill to tell the story of how Jesus died for our sins. Then add the tomb and stone to tell of His burial. Remove the stone as you tell how Jesus came to life again and won salvation for all, and that all who believe will have everlasting life (John 3:16).

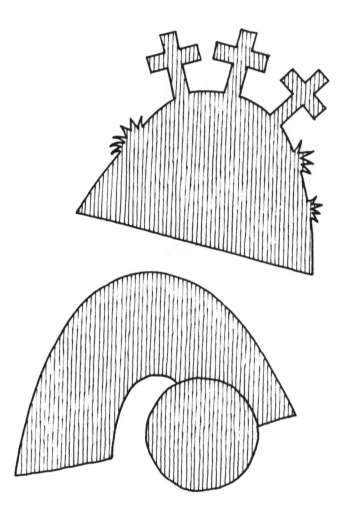

Shadow Puppet Patterns: Good Friday

Patterns may be used this size or enlarged to fit your needs.

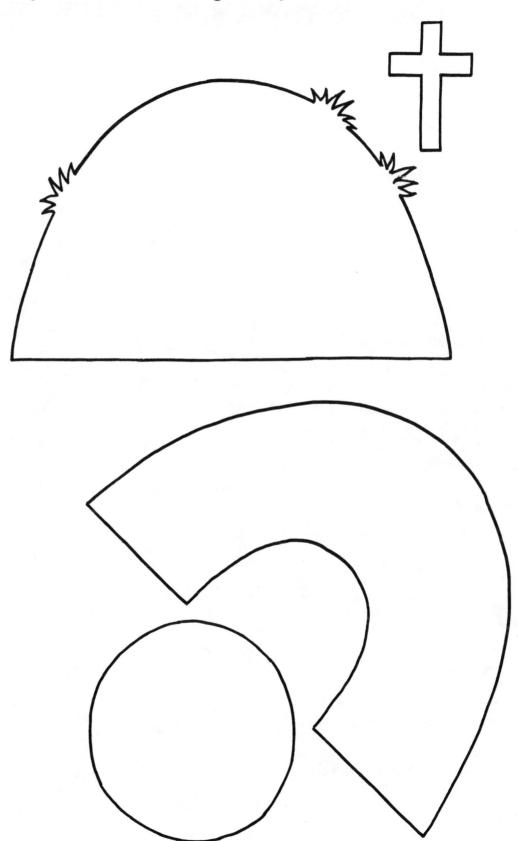

MARIONETTE PUPPET

What You Need

Poster board

Markers or crayons

Scissors

Glue

Yarn

Craft stick

Heavy cardboard

What You Do

1. Duplicate the pattern pieces on this page.

2. Trace the shapes onto poster board and cut them out.

3. Draw and color facial features and clothing.

4. Turn the puppet pieces face down and arrange them in order.

5. Glue yarn to the back of the pieces of the marionette as shown in the diagram so the arms, legs, head, and body are attached. Tie the yarn to the craft stick.

6. Cut and glue on a small piece of heavy cardboard behind each foot to serve as weights.

7. Move the craft stick to make your puppet move as you tell the Bible story.

More to Do

1. Make your own patterns.

2. Instead of thick cardboard, glue a button behind each foot.

Production Possibilities

· Use your marionette with small to medium groups, either over a table or in a stage with an open top.

> ⋮✧Marionette Puppet Pattern:
> Jesus Heals the Lame Man
>
> Patterns may be used this size or enlarged
> to fit your needs.

The Lesson Connection

Jesus Heals a Man by the Pool of Bethesda: John 5:2–11

Make two puppets, one to represent Jesus and the other to represent the lame man sitting by the pool. Use the puppets to act out the story as Jesus heals the lame man. Emphasize the drama by making the marionette walk and leap with joy. Invite the children to express their joy and praise for Jesus and His gift of love.

KITCHEN UTENSIL PUPPET

What You Need

Kitchen utensil
Movable eyes
Red felt

Scissors
Washable glue

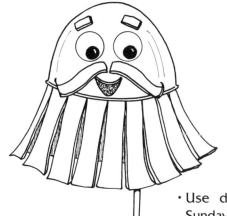

What You Do

1. Glue movable eyes on the kitchen utensil.

2. Cut a red mouth and glue it on.

3. Use the puppet to act out a story.

4. Wash off the eyes and mouth to convert the puppet back to a utensil.

More to Do

1. Glue on felt and yarn to add details to a permanent puppet.

2. Use a variety of household objects for puppets: feather duster, whiskbroom, spatula, large serving spoon, ladle, strainer, dustpan, broom, mop, etc.

3. Consider adding common accessories to your puppet—eyeglasses, scarf, hat, etc.

3. Tape a dowel stick to the utensil to convert it to a stick puppet.

4. Omit the mouth and add eyes only.

5. Add eyes made from felt or construction paper.

6. With a marker, draw eyes on white adhesive circles and stick on utensil.

Production Possibilities

- Depending on the utensil, puppets can be used for any size group.

- Hold puppets in your hand or behind a three-sided or card table stage.

- Use during a chapel talk, Sunday school opening, or for a lesson application.

The Lesson Connection

Abraham and Sarah: Genesis 18:1–15, 21:1–7

Use a whiskbroom for the Abraham puppet. Hold the whiskbroom with the straws going down to represent a beard. With heavy-duty tape, such as duct tape, attach a dowel to the back of the whiskbroom. Glue on two large craft eyes above the stitching. Use a feather duster to make the Sarah puppet. Hold the feather duster up by its handle. Glue eyes to the bottom half of the duster so the feathers form the hair. With duct tape, attach a dowel to the handle of the feather duster. Use a ladle for the Isaac puppet. Glue on two large craft eyes to the center of the back of the ladle. Attach a dowel to the handle with duct tape. Wrap a dishtowel or other cloth around the ladle to make it look like a baby in a blanket.

Have Abraham and Sarah tell part of the story of God showing His love for them by giving them Isaac. Have the puppets tell how they were visited by three strangers who predicted they would have a son. Hold up the Isaac puppet and tell what his name meant to Abraham and Sarah.

SLIDING PUPPET THEATER

What You Need

Shoebox   Scissors

Construction paper   Glue

Poster board   Ruler

Markers

What You Do

1. Cut one end from the box.

2. Use construction paper to make a background scene inside the box. Cut slits in the sides of the box.

3. Using the patterns on page 61, draw figures on poster board. Use a ruler to draw a connecting strip to the side of each figure. The strip should be longer than the width of the box.

4. Slide each strip through one of the slits.

5. Move the figures back and forth as you tell the story.

More to Do

1. Make figures from construction paper or draw them on a lighter-weight paper and glue cardboard or poster board behind them.

2. Decorate the outside of the box with wrapping paper.

3. Cut figures from old Sunday school leaflets or Bible story coloring books.

Production Possibilities

· Use a small box theater for a small-group presentation.

· Have each child make a sliding box theater to take home to use for sharing the Bible story with others.

The Lesson Connection

Easter Morning: John 20:1–18

Draw figures for Jesus, two women, and an angel at the tomb. Cut three slits in the sides of the box and insert the figures in the following order: angel/tomb toward the back, the two woman next, Jesus in front. Cut and glue a stand-up bush at the left side of the box, just in front of the Jesus figure. Hide the Jesus figure behind the bush until it is time in the story to bring Him out. Tell how Jesus rose on Easter to fulfill God's promise to send a Savior for the forgiveness of all sin.

Sliding-Tab Puppet Theater Patterns: Easter Morning

Patterns may be used this size or enlarged to fit your needs.

TUBE PUPPET THEATER

What You Need

Cardboard tube

Paper

Markers

Scissors

Glue

What You Do

1. Select a Bible story you can tell with a sequence of scenes or figures.

2. Cut strips of paper about 2½ inches longer than the width of the tube.

3. Draw a figure on the last 2 inches of each strip.

4. Glue the edge of the strip around the tube so it can turn around the tube.

5. As you tell the story, unwind the strips one-by-one to show the figure.

More to Do

1. Use toilet paper tubes for small tube puppets. Use paper towel tubes for taller puppets. Use oatmeal boxes for bigger figures.

2. Use crayons or colored pencils to draw the figures.

3. Cut figures from old Sunday school lessons or Bible coloring books to glue on for puppets.

Production Possibilities

• Use tube puppet theaters made from small tubes in small group settings. Use theaters made from bigger tubes with larger groups.

• Have children make a tube puppet theater to use to tell the story at home.

The Lesson Connection

The Coming of the Holy Spirit: Acts 2:1–13

Duplicate, color, and cut out the patterns for Peter and the flame. Fit the strips around a small tube. Use the tube puppet theater to tell the story of the coming of the Holy Spirit on the day of Pentecost. As an option, add a third strip for the people to whom Peter preached that day. Explain to the children that it was the Holy Spirit who helped Peter preach to more than 3,000 people that day. Remind them that it is the Holy Spirit who makes faith in our hearts and helps us tell others about Jesus.

Tube Puppet Theater Patterns: The Coming of the Holy Spirit

Patterns may be used this size or enlarged to fit your needs.

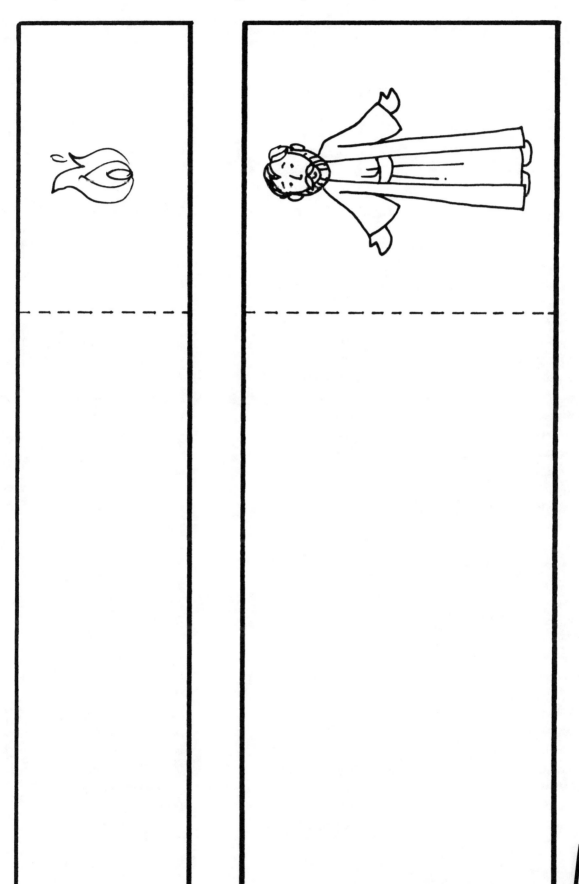

INDEX OF BIBLE STORIES